AMUSE-BOUCHES

Amuse-Bouches

Solee MacIsaac

EVERY BOOK PRESS

MMXXV

Book Design:

William Bentley

INTRODUCTION

Amuse-Bouches is a collection of thoughts written in Spring and Summer of 2024. The intent is to tantalize and stimulate interest in internal development for any and all who open the cover.

Solee MacIsaac

This work is dedicated to all my present and future readers, who stick with me through this journey.

Thank you: a big "Thank You" to William Bentley for all his work on my books. He does creative work on text layout and cover presentation. In other words, no books without William Bentley.

Sweet meats and lemon curd,
Herbs and spices,
Spark strong appetite.

AMUSE-BOUCHES

Petals were so heavy
On slender stems,
    Little heads dipped low.

Oh Earth,
We inhale you daily,
    Exhale you throughout night.

Fresh green veins
Run along fields
And deep into valleys.

Hearts burst golden white
In celebration
Of glorious Dawn.

Earth turns her shadowed face
Toward Sun,
Lavishing God's endless gift.

Birds ingesting small berries
Flit from bush to tree,
   Never minding bright sunlight.

Creatures of earth and air
Begin movement,
   Following life's demands.

Inside and outside
Have different rules,
   With similar conclusions.

Our unlimited perception
Through single eye
Can bring infinite joy.

Large white lilies
Along coastal road
Blaze their Spring triumph.

Only in temporal dark
Are we lost and afraid;
Full objective light is here.

One taste of real freedom
Engenders the
    Urgency to ascend.

Love, bittersweet,
Stands in the pathway;
    Don't neglect Home.

Take heart
A stone's throw,
    No farther.

Remove your slippers,
Feel earth between your toes,
　　Kiss breezes moving your lips.

Standing upright,
Being true to one's Self,
　　Requires truth, not self.

Life-giving streams
Run ahead and behind,
　　Saturating a thirsty world.

Seasons bring fresh lessons:
Replenished convictions,
    Although repeated, ever new.

Muse tickles and prods
'Til we respond
    And empty our cup.

Nothing is truly ours
For, truly,
    We need nothing.

Intoxicated by
Spring's perfume,
　　Thinking only of You.

Sweet William, Narcissus,
Wisteria, all climb
　　To Heaven's brink.

Beauty offers
Pleasure;
　　Truth gives a shock.

Coffee, morning,
Fresh eggs galore;
Waking up: delicious.

Cultures vary,
Essences reflect types,
Personalities compensate.

Deep in hidden caverns
Stalactites drip precious
Jewels from tip to tip.

Eye of the mind
Ever piercing
　　Inner shadows.

Self an illusion
Confronted
　　Repeatedly.

No beauty outside,
If no beauty
　　Inside.

There are no
Borders
    To reality.

Limitless, free
And unique,
    Looking for mirrors.

Gratifying
To see love grow
    In loved ones.

Edge of madness,
Edge of sanity,
Edges are the thing.

Fragrance penetrates
Inner experience
Without a whisper.

No finer raiment
Than a flower crown
On a present dome.

Loving attention
Outshines
    Gold.

Verdant fields
Perfume
    Valley dwellers.

Stars stare
Back at us:
    What do they see?

Are we curious
Explorers,
Unhappy to stay home?

Our true place
Has lonely views
Of our roaming misery.

Everything is still
And immovable
In the past.

We flit through
Past and future
    As if we truly exist:

Bypassing the present
In our misunderstood
    Imagination.

One step into the real,
So much fluff
    Blows away.

Grooming ourselves
For higher purposes involves
Deleting, not enhancing.

Beginnings excite;
Enduring to the finish,
Less so.

Old patterns
Not so simply dislodged,
Even by revelations.

Gratitude is hard won,
And easily lost,
    Through self-love.

A gracious mind and heart
Can travel the cosmos
    On love alone.

Ordinary objects
Make up our lives;
    Do we really see them?

If we are here to learn
And be tested,
　　Have we missed the lesson?

　　To love ourselves
And each other,
　　We must love the insignificant.

　　Wetted ground
Sprouts neon grass;
　　Bulbs push up blossoms.

Earth loves life,
All beings thrive
In heated frenzy.

Such a colorful array
For silent
Watchers.

Beauty of the blue angel
Sitting quietly
In the depth of her soul.

To truly see one angel
Is more than enough
To replenish an aching heart.

Sweet predawn light,
Melting night ghosts,
Embracing my strange longing.

Across the chasm
Our senses meet,
Limited knowing circulates.

A waterfall of love
Washes away
   Tears of neglect.

Anything can offer up its joy,
If brave enough
   To humbly join with it.

Water pearls
Adorn each leaf
   Sparkling in early light.

Heated passages
Through life
    Can melt away crusty oldness.

The cat being
Stares at me
    Through ancient eyes.

Old and young
Are meaningless
    In the upper ranges.

The gaze deepens
From a heart and mind
    Joined in compassion.

Flexing the heart muscle
Makes for a quick and strong
    Love response.

Inner light guides
Insight to boundaries
    Of higher realms.

Arrange the day
To meet yourself
At every turn.

Use the prismatic palette
To shade the love face
Beaming with Light.

To be allowed the sight
Of one angel
Is a rare and divine privilege.

Each elevated thought
Can assist climbing to the
    Pinnacle of No Thought.

Green: mixture of sun and sky
Covers the barren hills
    In velvet blankets.

A small whiff of heaven
Can awaken our senses
    To that which is beyond sense.

If Spring warblers
Are the harmonious appetizer,
Music is the main course.

Cacophonic applause
The ironic reward
For a sublime musical concert.

A well-trained ear
Participates
In the music.

The rhythm of love
Carries from heart
To heart.

Support pillars
Of high culture
Are superior virtues.

The real difference
Between humans
Is their being.

Tiny new leaves
Promise glorious
    Raiment in Summer.

Earth's beauty
Misleads the senses,
    By only hinting at reality.

Clear white and empty spaces
Do not need to be filled;
    Stretch out your Self at last.

Let my madness
Be divine,
    Let my heart be pierced.

Lowly creatures
Have much to teach
    Their "betters."

Moving swiftly over rolling hills
High flying swallow
    Spotted a perfect perch.

Ducks arrow north,
Returning from a southern
Vacation.

If everyone lived forever,
Would we take better care
Of our Earth?

So many who have passed
Have shown us the way;
Learning takes lifetimes.

The mind's Eye
Is a truth-seeking
    Missile.

This is the land of falsehoods;
In Reality
    Lies do not exist.

Beware hooded lovers,
Who come deep in the night:
    Your love is much too valuable.

With an open attitude,
Deeper degrees of presence
  Carry us further.

  To be as a child
Is a high state,
  Pure seeing, pure knowing.

  Rain hitting the roof, again,
Wet world is wetter;
  Streams run through the yard.

Spring has sprung a leak,
When it is drained
　　Sun will fill the coffers.

Radiant is the face
Of my lover,
　　Lighting mine in kind.

Watching the creek
Flow endlessly west;
　　A long journey to the sea.

Water and fire
Fascinate children and adults,
Incomprehensible gifts.

So much more so
The giver.
Can one comprehend a god?

Future scenarios spiral
Out before us—
Which will you choose?

Death is a constant,
We are meant to be temporary;
Life is a limited opportunity.

Ending life on Earth
Could mean beginning life
In a realm of different laws.

Love and light are tested,
Nothing stands a chance
Against You.

Fireplace roars into existence,
Damp rainy day won't win
In this house.

Tom turkey chased his lady
Down the driveway,
Spring-charmed exuberance.

When there is too much of me
In the way,
Little of value ensues.

Quiet morning light,
Steaming coffee,
    And you, Muse, start my day.

Look up,
Muddy ground will still be there;
    Deep blue sky is breaking through.

Timing in music follows
Artful laws that guide the ear
    To sublime and tragic states.

Visual laws guide the viewer
With color, light, and contrast,
Offering startling images.

Manipulation of the senses
Can produce strong effects,
Beyond usual experience.

Mastering art forms
Takes strenuous effort of will,
And touch of higher influence.

"Continue because you must"
Isn't an order;
    It's a lifeline.

There is no giving up,
Only,
    Letting down.

Blocking love
Is self-destruction,
    The very vehicle of salvation.

Sleeping body of Earth
Breathes, ingests, expels, and
Rolls over: tossing inhabitants.

Roles of men and women
Each have their denying force;
Beautiful: viva la différence.

The sweet pain of loving
Forges its way through us
To pull us home.

Without love and luck,
We are lost to chaos and crime:
    We, such impressionable stuff.

Savory, sweet, salty, bitter;
So many complex flavors
    Can awaken our stale palettes.

We are thrust into the unknown
Daily, nightly, every moment;
    Aware only when brave enough.

Bodies are finite,
Fragile and perishable,
Unlike eternal Self.

A seed grows
Even if neglected;
There is no alternative.

The enduring
Heart
Has wings.

Strip down, crawl through
Crack between door and floor
Of so-called life.

Rain again, unbidden,
Except by the tulips,
Who wholeheartedly accept.

Liquid Spring
Gushes forth in wild abandon,
Wetting Earth's dry throat.

Surprise! Snowy April Fools,
Powdery white,
        Dusting flowers with crystals.

Fear freezes,
Envy sickens,
        Love melts.

New surprise! Earthquake!
This day doesn't quit.
        Uneasy ground vibrations.

Watch!
Slow wits
    Breed deviation.

Lavender days,
Purple twilights,
    Indigo nights.

Spend less time ruminating,
Spend more time
    Really existing.

Woke up grumpy,
Difficult to be grateful,
When grumbling.

Spectacular view
With eyes cleansed
Of self-opinions.

The immediacy
Of higher Self appearing
Is an intimate experience.

No judgement,
No worry,
No "No."

What color is Love?
Prismatic light
Beaming from warm eyes.

When friendship
Encounters obstacles,
Leap very high over them.

Words can be
Fierce enforcers,
    Or softer than fleece.

O, Beauty—
Don't leave so soon;
    Stay 'til sleep conquers me.

The fiery whirl
Receives a shroud today,
    Making the world weep.

Things are
Ordinary,
Only when we are.

Change happens
Continually;
Transformation, seldom.

The viewer behind the eyes
Sees inner vision,
Which colors his view.

Outside time,
Sequential forever
    Has no meaning.

    Resistance is futile,
Let reality
    In.

    Resisting is persistent;
It is not a way of life,
    But a way of death.

Surrender to love,
Open all the doors,
Light up the house.

Sing Yes!
Dance Yes!
Swallow Yes whole.

You, accepter of all,
Bend to my lowly station,
Grace me with your light.

Face to face,
We meet beneath
Weeping wisteria.

Great is our ardor,
Small is our wisdom,
Brutal is our destiny.

Do you hear the knocking?
Someone wants in…
Or, wants us to appear.

Peeling back the layers,
The center is nothing,
Which is the best part.

The tasty bit that excites
Is food for thought,
Not stomach.

Earth light is splendid,
Cosmic light is majestic,
Uncreated light is divine.

The rain stops,
Sun appears ever new,
  Warming hearts everywhere.

Taking a wrong turn
Doesn't mean going in circles,
  Turning back is possible.

A lifetime of changes,
Yet something remains
  The same.

Gracious and serene,
A generous heart
    Contains universal love.

Words spoken
Are weightier
    Than those written.

If your happiness depends
Upon lucky accidents,
    Odds are against you.

Doors of life's dark prison
Dissolve
In the clear light of reality.

Complexities of living
Simplify
In the present moment.

The smallest thing
Can be the most difficult:
To breathe in the moment.

Relinquish your imaginary
Control;
All will be as it should be.

Judgement:
Reacting to a small mistake,
Is a mistake.

Interruption
Of our momentum
Is a great gift.

We are drawn to what is
Good and beautiful,
    As tastes become more refined.

In a higher world
All is beautiful,
    Because it exists.

A rest, a meal,
Friends gather in the evening
    For a glass of wine.

Not everything is fair,
Even so, good is increased;
    Love is a strong force.

Burden of a woman
To that of a man is thrice:
    Carrying hers, his and their child.

Men and women both suffer
The burden of society's
    Extravagant emotional waste.

There is much
To process and transform,
Fuel for ascending souls.

To be above the mundane
Requires more love
Than is normally allotted.

Great poets and philosophers
See more light than most,
Our fate relies on outside help.

Blessings come in many forms;
We can be blessings blind
    And rue our best chances.

Obstinate and dull,
The bull treads his way
    Through lovely flowered fields.

It may be painful,
Keeping your eye open for so long:
    Required payment for love.

Children, soft and innocent,
Turn into untried people,
With their own silent star.

Pressures pull apart
Our finer sensibilities;
Transforming allows union.

There are no opposites
When uncreated light
Reveals inner union.

Heaven's architecture
Must be beautiful,
    With no need for security.

Laws of this level
Require air, food, and water;
    Next level has other needs.

Gods are nothing,
If not
    Organized.

The higher up you are,
Clearer air provides
　　Expanded view, finer breath.

We help each other a lot,
But the most needed assistance
　　Comes in much different forms.

Our true Self
Will appear,
　　When higher Will wills.

Nothing so perfect
As a fresh apple,
	Straight from the tree.

Fragrant and gorgeous,
Spring orchards
	Lift spirits universally.

A new day
Greets my eyes
	With unlimited beauty.

Bounty of Mother Earth
Provides physical sustenance
For all its life forms.

We have needs beyond
Nature's gifts,
        As we are made of stardust.

Luminous green
Crashes through my window;
        Spring creations are relentless.

Never prepared enough
To receive so much
    Resplendence.

With more receptivity,
More appears to
    Receive.

If you are holier than thou,
Are you really
    Holy?

To keep a gracious mind,
It is essential
To remember blessings.

Gratitude is hard won,
And easily
Misplaced.

Sacrifice is a useful tool,
But is not equal to
Suffering.

Do not rush to fill a vacancy;
The silent space within
    Is sacred.

Love appears in many forms,
None so bittersweet
    As watching a child suffer.

Precious life affords
Limited chances to
    Realize what is not us.

Willingly we cover our face
Hiding from our real Self,
As if we could.

Help from beyond our sphere
Graciously peels dead leaves
From our flowering soul.

Wounds heal,
Scars fade,
What is left, endures.

The core of each of us
Is unblemished:
    Leave what is not you behind.

The Gods know
What we need,
    And humbly give their best.

Impossible to comprehend
Such sublime servitude
    For such a high purpose.

Love from higher beings
Is more than we can absorb
Or understand.

Senses and thoughts
May be only properties
Of this gross level.

What amazing subtleties
Will accompany our
Bodiless existence?

Our position
In the wild scheme of things
Is below most of the universe.

Such potential
Locked inside small beings;
Where is the key?

Six swans
Fly home
On sunset wings.

Focusing on flaws
Can help at the beginning,
But ultimately retards progress.

Staying internally home,
Letting all come to us,
Removes unnecessary strain.

Good is what brought you here,
Better is what you practice,
Best is here now.

A lonely horse
Under a striped sky
    Munches strands of new grass.

It's lilac and tulip
Time of year;
    What could be more beautiful.

Mana from heaven
Sustains
    All who accept reality.

Following the path of beauty
Enhances a life
    Of pursuing refinement.

A small taste
Opens senses,
    Promising culinary pleasure.

French flavors grace
The dining table
    Of a discerning gourmand.

The right thing,
At the right time,
Shines in perfect harmony.

The melody is sweet,
While the symphony
Is complex and delicious.

Songs carry emotions
Through a journey
Of joy, memory, and longing.

There is a reason angels are
Depicted with instruments,
　　As perfect music is heaven.

We aspire to be more than
Ourselves;
　　To be more, we must be less.

Be kind to yourself,
You spend the most time with
　　You.

On gravel road,
Blonde girl tenderly caresses
   White horse.

You, who are not visible,
Enchant my ear
   With intimate musings.

Following upslope,
While lagging behind,
   Ahead You dissolve in clouds.

A jamboree of wildflowers
Challenges the eye
    With a parade of opulence.

The greatest good
Outshines
    The adequate.

A small dew drink
From a tiny petal
    Splashes cool a baby ant.

Difficult to perceive
Beyond this dimension
    With only two eyes.

Without luck
A seed will not
    Sprout.

A hand up
Is sometimes difficult
    To discern.

Being small is good,
Unless you imagine
You are tall.

Here we reside
In the now,
Everlasting.

Our true home
Always
Awaits us.

In a bouquet
Of beautiful flowers
    The greenery sets the stage.

    The present is the only place
Where things
    Can actually happen.

Drop guilt;
Remorse may help to fuel
    Being here, now.

What is our significance?
To merge into
Nothing.

The poetry of higher beings
Has produced the beautiful
Nature of Earth.

Coconut, lemon, cherries;
What delicious tastes
Offered by amazing trees.

Foolish to equate
Creativity and control,
    As all flows as it will.

Small birds rise as one,
When my cat
    Appears.

Full sun
Fills the garden
    Humming with bees.

The very center
Of my being
        Humbly, thanks You.

Even though
The god guides your moves,
        Results are your own.

Target practice improves skill.
Unless you are graced,
        Consistent bullseyes doubtful.

Slanting rays
Penetrate dark forest,
    Spotlighting clump of wild iris.

Secrets are an illusion
Too expensive
    For an ascending soul.

Giving where needed
Is love shared
    And multiplied.

Each step is numbered,
Don't skip
Any.

Eternal light
Holds everything
In shining reality.

How things look,
Depends upon
Inner attitudes.

How things really look,
Depends upon
    Core essence.

Lewis Carroll's
Through the looking glass
    Sees topsy-turvy reality.

Sun sinks below Earth's edge,
Preceded by
    Blazing celebration of color.

Established religion
Teaches society
Morals and virtues.

Practical maps that teach
Spiritual transformation
Are scarce.

Help each other
Through the life maze.
Ignite each other's flame.

The thirsty valley
Calls to the lofty mountain,
   "Let the water fall!"

We are where we are,
Because
   We are where we are.

Learning to let go the reins
May be scary,
   But the horse knows the way.

Time to trust
All that has gone before:
    Supplied perfect positioning.

We are free to exist,
Free to enter reality,
    Free to experience and create.

How far down must we dig
To reach lifeblood of Earth,
    Ageless rivers of gold.

Throbbing heart of Earth,
Too loud for us to hear,
   Sends booms through the universe.

We don't need
Greater intelligence;
   Pursue a fuller heart.

Endless pervasive light
Delineates all
   In eternal existence.

Dance in moonlight
To the harmonic beauty
Of star symphony.

To perceive more
Than human vision allows,
Defer to your soul's eye.

Visiting my hand,
Lady bug spreads wings
And flees to windowsill.

Similar molecules resonate,
Hearts sing and rumble with
　　Laughter from deep down.

None so heavy
As the guilt and regret
　　We carry.

How to measure value?
Length, breadth, duration.
　　Search for objectivity.

We aspire to what we value;
We are fortunate
        To value our Selves.

Worriers
Don't need or want
        Legitimacy.

Torches light
From each other
        Running from shore to home.

Descending into the
Deep canyon
 We spy the lighted chateau.

As one, we sing
A song of gratitude,
 Welcoming coming rest.

Travelers shoulder
Necessities
 Until journey's end.

Church spires, electric cars,
Windmills, computer phones.
Times feel uneven.

A spectacular day,
Heralding a harmonious
Evening with friends.

Hardship comes
To everyone,
Not all use it.

Dandelion makes
A good umbrella,
　　If you are an aphid.

Swimming upstream
Isn't easy;
　　Reward makes all worthwhile.

Loving may stretch us;
Worry not,
　　Our shape is retained.

Genuine and sincere
Go a long way towards
Grateful and accepting.

Flaming light
On a red-leafed tree
Caught my beauty-craving eye.

Love holds
The best
Of me.

The light like no other
Is always there,
    Even in our darkest moments.

Keeping aware of the
Moment's offering
    Enables heightened existence.

Sweet celebrations
Of birthday anniversaries
    Acknowledge milestones.

Life has first moments,
And last moments,
    In between is this moment.

Are you the memory
Of your future self?
    Of course not, You is only now.

There is nothing to lose:
Invest in your higher Self
    By forsaking everything else.

A light rain
Refreshes
    Every vivid color.

Great composers of the past
Still send their message:
    Harmony and love.

That chortling baby is still
Inside us,
    Having a chuckle at our foibles.

Cascading layers
Of lightest light
Surround a budding soul.

In Paradise,
The highest artists
Are Heaven's light-weavers.

Cry for a Muse
To bring forth creations
That light up a barren heart.

A life contains many things,
All of which
    Bring one to this very instant.

The world provides
Many varied opportunities
    For higher centers to consume.

Standing on the threshold,
Enter in and leave outside
    What belongs out there.

Everywhere is the place
To receive every offering
Of the Gods.

Contradictions imply
Comparisons between
Different situation levels.

Developments take
Their own time,
Realizations need no time.

The present moment
Is not a pinnacle of experience,
    It is the only way to experience.

When there is a hush,
What do the birds know
    That we don't?

Spring seems softer
Than the other seasons,
    Delicate tender new growth.

The days slip by,
But the moment
        Can last forever.

It is easy to love the beautiful,
More difficult to accept
        That we are worthy of love.

Egypt, Persia, Greece:
Each has their Sun time,
        And eventually crumble.

To be home
Ruby slippers
Are not necessary.

Early morning sunlight
Slants across the garden,
Showcasing humble vegetables.

Flavor intensifies
With color
And aroma.

Everything eats,
Bodies replenish
By transforming fuel.

Impressions are
Transformed
Into understandings.

Life is supported
By continuing processes;
Interchanges within biosphere.

Appearing suddenly
On the scene,
As if given a sparkling gift.

So many colorful
Fruits and vegetables,
Gardening labor fills bellies.

Embrace your life
Whatever it contains;
Experiences are valid teachers.

Our precious attention
Focused with love
Unexpectedly changes things.

A carrot draws the donkey,
We are easily led by
Promises of wealth, affection.

Unfortunately,
We are not always grateful
When reality invades imagination.

A full stomach
Waylays
    Worries and fears.

Whether things
Are good or bad
    Depends upon perspective.

True generosity
Comes from the heart,
    Not the wallet.

Water quenching new growth,
Rain again,
A last big gulp before Summer.

Whistling in the distance,
An eerie sound through the fog,
A ghost train clatters by.

When entering sacred space,
Remove your slippers,
Tread softly, be a prayer.

Love in its many forms
Can be slow or brutally fast,
    Leaves little space for the trivial.

In an instant,
Here we are and
    Love surrounds us.

The permeable truth
Becomes false
    At the next level up.

Don't forget
To see your
Nose.

Some forces—
Love, light, consciousness—
Pass across dimensions.

Nameless conscious
Nothingness
Only LIGHT.

Spring holds a special secret;
Much is revealed in beauty,
   In the unseen even more so.

Do we wobble at times?
Toddlers in the higher worlds
   Are learning.

Tears can't cleanse
A messy kitchen,
   Time for a mop.

Look to your longing,
You can have it all:
Now.

Trees are Earth, Air and Sun,
With water lubricant,
Just like us.

Happy met,
Face to face,
Joy unbounded.

So much wanting,
When You were here
All along.

Though I can't see it,
I know your spirit face
So well.

Is there life after life?
Only if there is life
Now.

Velvet petals line the pathway,
Follow heavenly music,
    Be in the scene.

Graceful and kind,
Full of love
    And soft kisses.

Magnets attract
And repulse
    Simultaneously.

Aligned electrons, like love,
Are immaterial,
But carry energetic force.

Empathy for friend's sorrow
Is not uncommon,
Reviving their presence is.

Being together
Exchanging glances
Filled with love.

Watching the daylight fade
Memories invade,
    Ushering in the long past.

A friendly voice
Is a retrieval
    From the unreal.

Dinner is cooking,
Time for a palate catalyst:
    Amuse bouche.

Diamonds on the lake
Chasing the fleeing
   Blue heron.

Expectations
Unfulfilled
   Provide opportunities.

The view from Third Eye
Is neither lofty nor tragic:
   A visual penetration of reality.

Many experiences are
Repetitive,
But not for higher centers.

Emotions run high
When pressure is applied,
But love is stronger than fear.

Love and Graciousness,
Twin sisters,
Stronger than Hercules.

Health is essential,
Especially sans blockages
    To love.

    We toast in appreciation
To those who have
    Touched our hearts.

Candlelight
Creates deep shadows,
    But has a lovely glow.

There is more to
Be
Than to know.

Kindness serves others
While gracing
Ourselves.

Watching ourselves
Drop old accounts
Freshens a feeling of life.

The first bite
After a fast
    Is an exquisite taste.

Raise a glass
To ever-renewing life,
    With a large splash of love.

Some experiences
Take more time to understand
    With positivity and patience.

I am here,
And then,
I am not.

Consistency is important;
More important,
Accepting fluctuations.

Pickles and profiteroles
Are food,
But don't make a dinner.

Thinking is good,
Doing is better,
 Being is best.

One toe peeking out of suds,
Warm bubbles soaking
 All worries away.

Growth in nature
Reaffirms health of Earth,
 Cycles continue in perpetuity.

Gentle and serene,
She floats over fields,
Airy Will-o-the-Wisp.

Day is here, again,
Time and Nature consistently
Spin our planet.

Anything done
Without love
Is not worth doing.

Love in the open air
Is our existence,
    Pure and simple.

My dreams include a pencil,
Symbol is…
    To keep writing?

Love links and bonds us
To the highest
    In each other.

The carousel of sleep
Spins round and round,
Dare to step off.

We are the support system
For those who
Come after us.

Joining to celebrate
A holiday
Promotes joyous presence.

Daily labor:
Payment for sustenance;
    All of worth requires payment.

Payment for
Higher values
    Difficult to determine.

Trust in deeper understandings
To weather storms of
    Doubt.

We need each other
To keep our heads
    Above murky waters.

An empty mind
Can sometimes lead to
    A full heart.

Support from others
Is essential, and also illusory,
    As all are one.

The storm passes,
But nothing really changes,
Until we do.

Closer than your own hand,
Infinite reality
Awaits your awareness.

Guard your impulses
With wisdom,
Until perfect alignment.

Spring melts into Summer,
Green into gold,
Mist into glare.

Delicate strands
Of corn silk
Draped from counter's edge.

Ordinary things
Speak up when we
Listen.

Molding pie dough,
Optimistically anticipating
The ultimate result.

Hot tea at day's end
Soothes worn nerves
And tired muscles.

Sun rays piercing clouds,
Morning cool before heat rise,
Small birds pecking at ground.

The only thing that you can
Give more of, more than you have,
Is love.

Wild mint, green and fresh,
Growing along the creek side,
Fragrant and enticing.

A beautiful day
Frames my state,
Love needs no introduction.

Slow down,
Become stillness,
    To catch up to the moment.

The chalice of forgiveness
Is proffered to those to
    Whom remorse is shown.

In town: bewildering array
Of confusing things,
    For which there is no desire.

To lead a simple life,
Shed all unnecessary,
Embrace joy.

Red roses are necessary,
Priorities change
With emotional development.

Loving Self
Extends love
To everyone and everything.

Musical instruments
Are pleasant to look at,
    More so to hear played well.

Melodies can elevate
Our state,
    And harmonize our being.

Sunlight is strong,
Starlight is subtle,
    Uncreated light is eternal.

Kitchen aromas tantalize,
If you cook it,
They will come.

The days are long,
The heat is high,
We are cooking nicely.

The Fountain of Life
Is all-giving
Until the claim of Death.

The prickly side of loving
Is watching
  The belovéd suffer.

New kitten fluffy soft,
Black and white,
  Eyes bright.

Golden madrone
Drooping in the heat,
  Shelter for small birds.

Although travel can educate,
Staying home
Reveals much more.

Sit quietly,
Silence the heart,
Know your true Self.

Hunger outshines
The tastiest
Appetizer.

Wildlife
Does not imply
    Wild living.

Grounded in the moment,
Welcoming all,
    The Self nourishes its Self.

It's nice to be here,
In the place of my birth,
    The inner temple.

Green runners
With curling tendrils
        Cover dark-shaded ground.

        Look before you leap,
But leap
        Anyway.

        Take a heady draft
Of Love,
        Intoxicate your Self.

When the lines blur
Between the worlds,
    Jump through the cracks.

Feel with your head,
Think with your heart,
    Speak with your eyes.

Self-righteous attitudes
Will soon be humbled
    By self-examination.

The edge of Summer
Races forward
In heated waves.

Let go of yourself,
You won't be lost,
We will all be enhanced.

Our marigold Sun
Sends nourishing rays
Freely to all on Earth.

We are not capable
Of the love
    We are showered with.

To outshine
The Sun,
    Dissolve in uncreated light.

Feeling your love
Supports my day,
    Ups and downs don't matter.

We are lucky
Air is heavy
        Lest it dissipate into ether.

        Beautiful, clean and pure
Describe
        Uncreated light.

        It is a joy to breathe,
Smile at this day,
        And mean it.

Mid-June celebrates
The flowering season,
    Weddings abound.

Hang on to your hat
For a wild ride
    Down the mountain side.

Don't war with
Gravity,
    It always wins.

Eat your fill,
Fuel your body,
Not your waistline.

Fame and fortune
Are found by few,
Fewer still find uncreated light.

Each moment
Carries a possibility
For dimensional adventure.

A beam of white light
Marks the entrance
    To eternity.

The closer you look,
Details appear in an
    Undreamt landscape.

From the ocean's bottom
To the galaxy rim,
    We thrive.

Walk together
Into unknown
        Territory.

        Is this a low-producing
God
        Factory?

        Great swathes of June's colors
Lay across rich fields;
        Bee heaven.

Payment is incomprehensible
For the incredible privilege
    Of our lives in presence.

Lovely being
Creates
    Sweet environment.

Grace in adversity
Is rare,
    And much relished.

A tasty morsel
Can invite appetite,
  And begin the entire banquet.

Water-loving lotus
Rises purely
  From mucky bottom.

Silent and serene
A graceful geisha
  Trails fingertips through pond.

Small bites
Add up to
    An entire melon.

Intentional dining
Allows ingesting food and
    Impressions simultaneously.

Profound thoughts,
Not as cherished
    As childlike presence.

Viewing the invisible
Contradicts eyesight;
Requires Third Eye.

A sip of spicy wine;
Nuanced flavors swirl
The educated palate.

Feather light,
A loving caress of soft lips
Crosses my brow.

Small and simple,
Quiet and humble,
   Does not imply insignificant.

Heart of my heart
Brimming over
   With rosy love for You.

Graceful and elegant,
Reality outclasses
   Sophistication.

Resistance means
We are not ready
        For the final lesson.

        Willingness to accept
What is presented,
        Indicates readiness.

        Look long and deep
Into the eyes
        Of the belovéd.

Midsummer nights
Are short,
    Moon dance while you can.

Being here in this moment
Love circulates,
    Presence is beyond value.

Our planet Earth
Frames our mortality
    Until we reach our real home.

Your arms surround
My frazzled state,
　　Even though transparent.

She dances so lightly,
Barely touching earth,
　　Her gown pearlescent white.

There is love everywhere
We look;
　　Without love we cannot live.

To see one's own love
Reflected back from the world
    Is tremendous reinforcement.

A lit candle
Shows little shine
    In broad daylight.

When in love,
Your face literally
    Lights up.

Not everything
Worth knowing
    Can be proven.

Kindness has a way
Of returning
    To the sender.

A hint of smokey taste
Is in the air,
    Barbecue season is here.

June races out
With her rose garment
    Trailing into July's sauna.

A small bite,
Savory and spicy,
    Melts into taste buds.

A pyramid of light
Points to the stars,
    Citizens of the Milky Way.

Trends are changeable,
Classics remain
As icons of style.

Shiny objects
Appeal to senses,
Symbols of invisible treasure.

Ingredients for a tasty snack
Are nurtured and grown
With loving attention.

Time is a cruel master
But a patient
    Amalgamator.

Preference
May define particulars,
    Irrelevant with scale.

Dance to celebrate
Midyear point,
    Cherish this very moment.

Sweetest taste
Is but for a moment,
    Sweetest soul takes lifetimes.

Yellow roses fill the room
With sunshine,
    And exquisite fragrance.

Sublime state of grace
Teaches
    Humility.

Bend low
To raise up
   A tiny child of wonder.

Senses define our world,
But do they
   Really?

Large gaps
Remain between
   The boundaries of our senses.

Mistakes made
Are not the problem;
Repeated ones are tormentors.

Exotic spices tantalize;
Good old-fashioned
Meat and potatoes satisfy.

Kitchen aromas
Encourage mouth watering
And stomach growling.

Bathe in the forever light
Of unearthly radiance,
Immerse yourself in reality.

What finer energies
Become
Food for Gods?

Feeling your presence,
In every nook and corner,
Loneliness is abandoned.

Become as large
As the air surrounding you,
As bright as sunlight.

Help is needed,
And given,
Though not always recognized.

Being true to oneself,
Requires awareness
Of one's Self.

Red roses cluster
About silver-throated
    Hummingbirds.

A whiff of perfume
From invisible paradise
    Catches attention and is gone.

Rain is predicted,
And never comes,
    Lost droplets on the wind.

Being grateful for a life
Of lessons learned
　　Is a gift in itself.

So many breaths,
So many beats,
　　Then it is finished.

The view from your eyes
Is unique;
　　Perceive wisely.

True caring
Isn't saccharine sweet,
But committing with heart.

To release what isn't needed
In the moment
Is more difficult than it seems.

A pleasant interlude
Much sought after;
Available in an eye blink.

A lick on the cone
Won't stop the melting,
But fun anyway.

Being together,
Being grateful,
Being shared.

Absolute perfection
Does not exist
On this level.

Know that
You are loved
    More than you can love.

Never underestimate
What holds you close
    In loving arms.

Heat coming in tsunami
Not mere waves,
    Fricassee weather.

To elevate
One's state,
Serve the highest.

Pick up your skirts,
Flammable dry brambles
Will alight from your light.

Everything comes
In its time,
Rushing will only rush yourself.

Children ask simple questions,
Often not so simply answered;
    We know less than we think.

Another day is counted
In the long chain of events
    That leads to final destination.

Swans with heads bowed
Swim in unison
    Across sapphire lake.

If we had to count our
Blessings,
　　　Infinity is a big number.

Tiny capsule of time
Holds precious potential:
　　　Enter eternity through this gate.

Night closes one in,
Tremors and fancies
　　　Dance beneath lids.

Alchemically sound,
Love and light
Heal.

Bodies may not endure,
Who you are
Remains eternally.

Worms provide silk,
Bees their honey,
Gods uncreated light.

Beauty is really
An amazing state
Of grace.

The emotional eye
Sees more beauty
Than all it beholds.

Her tresses
Flutter in the Summer breeze,
She floats cloud-like over all.

Swim into the warm embrace
Of every mother's love
Throughout time and history.

Unravel your clenched
And knotted psyche,
Open your heart to love.

Drink deep:
The well of truth
Will never run dry.

Craving spiritual growth
Can attract a peculiar play
By design.

Cool water
In much demand;
Springs generously supply.

Summer's roaring heat
Rushes down the valley,
Baking foliage in its wake.

Carousel of life spins round
Chasing itself endlessly
On the same level.

To enter in,
Leave the mind to rest,
Open the heart with eye.

One penny
Can be enough
To purchase the world.

The land is strange,
Stranger still,
The visiting stranger.

Days of love and joy
Stretching before us,
Wondrous and light filled.

A garden of delights
Awaits a world-weary soul
At journey's end.

Orpheus with his lyre
Guided followers
On a musical odyssey.

One sweet tone
Mystifies listeners,
An opening to brilliance.

The strength
Of solid light
Confounds the senses.

Sunlight is
Amuse bouche
For holy light.

A distant call
On night wind
Haunts late hour dreams.

Ideal life in a city of light;
Ancient Greeks dreamed it best,
Who lives it?

Seasons continue
Each with their own beauty
And adversities.

Every culture's tastes vary,
Favorite dishes of healthy food
Will please some, repel others.

Hunger
Is beyond
Preference.

We, the eyes and hands
Of Gods,
Honor our highest use.

Particles of light
Infuse our being
Until we are weightless.

We are lifted
To greet the Gods
On the day assigned at birth.

Grasses shrivel
Under July's sun,
    Kitty seeking shade.

Pink and white blossoms
Surround the doorway
    Where the belovéd lives.

We are so lucky
To be part of the growth
    Of the conscious soul.

Your smile enlightens
Every face
And every heart.

Awareness and realization,
Keys
That open inner doorways.

We are helped
In ways
That we cannot imagine.

A huge part of living
Are those
You share it with.

Spread your golden skirt
Upon the green,
Relish each opening blossom.

Our light-filled sky
Hides those night diamonds,
Which peek out at dusk.

We are sustained
By Love-driven Will,
Undetectable by our senses.

A whiff of reality
Can entice or alarm,
Or, amazingly, both.

How to value
A budding soul,
Priceless and invisible.

The light of all light
Emanates eternally
From itself.

Nothing is ever
Truly learned
Without living it.

Not the body, brain nor mind
Ascends to ultimate reality;
Soul alone attains high spirit.

Summer nights, blessedly cool,
Spill waves of love
From starlight to eye glimmers.

To overcome bodily wants,
Focus on higher needs,
Say "Yes" to serving upwards.

Voices upraised in joy
Play upon the ear
In harmonious delight.

Song without words
Conveys more
    Than a library of thoughts.

Holiday decor garnishes
Banquet hall
    Awaiting honored guest.

You've lived with black and white
For long enough;
    Ease into the world of color.

Time and distance
Are not barriers
To the flow of love or light.

To withdraw and intentionally
Cloister for a spell
Can provide deeper insights.

The milky river of stars
Shines night and day,
Even when we can't see it.

Accept the lily bouquet
So sweetly offered
By Pharaoh's daughter.

Ancient peoples live in time;
Curtains between dimensions
Are drawn back in eternity.

From Mount Olympus
Look back on your present,
Rejoice that you are here!

The feathered fan
Wafts jasmine breezes
Across cooling skin.

Honeyed nuts and dates
Tempt eyes and tastebuds;
Gaze across the Nile.

At last,
Trumpets announce
The Bark of Ra's arrival.

Savory and bitter-sweet
Lifetimes
  Feed the soul with lessons.

www.ingramcontent.com/pod-product-compliance
Lightning Source LLC
Chambersburg PA
CBHW021625120626
46545CB00002B/403